THANKSGIVING LETTERS
1974-1995

WILLIAM H. DANFORTH

Elizabeth Gray and William H. Danforth, September 1994

To all my friends and co-workers whose vision, energy, ability, and generosity made possible the modern Washington University; and most especially to Elizabeth Gray Danforth, my partner in life and partner in building our beloved institution.

WILLIAM H. DANFORTH

Chancellor William H. Danforth with a group of freshmen, September 1971

For 21 years, Bill Danforth sent a letter each Thanksgiving to "the many friends who make Washington University possible." The letters touched on events of the year, highlighted things he had been reading or thinking, and explored the role of universities in the world. Above all, these were letters of thanks—thanks for Washington University and for the people who made it such a special place.

For so many of us and for such a long time, Bill and his late wife, Ibby, have embodied this institution. They have had an extraordinary impact on the past, present, and future of the University. We cherish this association and the letters that have become one of Bill's many gifts to the Washington University family. We now express our thanks to him for his enduring dedication to this institution and for the immeasurable ways in which he has inspired the Washington University community for more than five decades. Here, for the many friends of Washington University, are Bill Danforth's Thanksgiving Letters.

MARK S. WRIGHTON
14TH CHANCELLOR
WASHINGTON UNIVERSITY IN ST. LOUIS
1995–

During his 24-year tenure as Chancellor of Washington University, William H. Danforth received many tributes for his steady leadership, his extraordinary vision, and his tireless efforts to build a local institution into an internationally recognized university. Yet amid these accolades, there was little mention of one treasure trove that he left to us: a series of annual letters, written from 1974 to 1995, that have become known as the "Thanksgiving letters."

Each summer, when Bill and his beloved wife Ibby gathered with family at their Michigan vacation home, Bill created one of the letters found in these pages. He intended them as letters of appreciation to alumni and friends for their interest in and contributions to the school. However, they have since lived on as timeless, thought-provoking, inspirational messages.

The first letter came in 1974, and through the following years, the ideas that Bill expressed frequently sparked discussion among recipients like my husband and me, both Washington University alumni. People unfamiliar with the letters became interested; they asked to read them and have copies. Soon they became the springboard for meaningful conversations all around St. Louis. It is no wonder that requests to see them compiled into a book have continued through the years. Now, at last, we have our "jewels" in book form.

When we relish each letter one by one, and take the time to reflect upon it, we find ourselves asking such questions as: "How can my life be more meaningful?" "Am I ignoring an opportunity that would allow me to help?" "Are my eyes, ears, and heart open to needs around me that I haven't taken time to notice?" For in these letters, we meet a man who always has time to listen, who views situations from others' perspectives, whose thinking is inclusive, and whose actions follow careful evaluation—not hasty judgment.

It has been my privilege to re-read these letters in preparation for writing this preface. Once again, I am inspired by this remarkable man whose wisdom, values, and vision lift my own thinking to a higher level and who challenges me to examine my own ideas. It naturally followed that, under his leadership, Washington University continued to grow into an institution not only of the highest academic caliber but also of trust, integrity, and family feeling.

The jewels that Chancellor Danforth has given us in these pages can help each of us discover ourselves. They also give us the opportunity to share his stimulating thoughts with others. I hope you enjoy them as much as I have.

MARIE PRANGE OETTING
AB '49
CHAIR, ALUMNI BOARD OF GOVERNORS
2001-2002

*Washington University freshmen with William H. Danforth
at the Chancellor's picnic,* August 1973

"...Reading has been a passion of mine at least since early adolescence. Books written by others have added to my knowledge and shaped my under-standing of the world and the people who inhabit it. Insights elegantly and forcefully phrased have locked into my mind, helped form my character, and stayed with me for decades. They come to mind in difficult times or when I try to put something new to my experience in its proper place and perspective.

"I wish that I were a writer. Then I could pass on what I most value to intelligent people of my generation and generations coming after. I would not ask for a wide readership, just a few who would resonate to the same things that I consider to be beautiful and true. That would be a way of giving back to the world, to give to others what so many writers have given to me. There could be no better legacy. A well-written book can be a kind of immortality.

"If you think I am caught up with romantic notions, you are probably right, but that is the way I am and that is the way I see writing a book. I honor those who report their own truths, often laboriously and even painfully gained, who do so in their own style and so create something lasting. It is a privilege to be among those of the Washington University faculty who write books."

WILLIAM H. DANFORTH
13TH CHANCELLOR
WASHINGTON UNIVERSITY IN ST. LOUIS
1971-1995
excerpt from Faculty Book Celebration speech, December 4, 2003

THANKSGIVING LETTERS
1974-1995

1974 The fall semester started well. The freshmen and many of their parents arrived on campus in late August. On paper, the new students were bright and able. About half had finished in the top 10 percent of their high school class. In person, they were attractive and enthusiastic. They came from diverse backgrounds and from all over the country.

When the students were asked why they had picked Washington University, their answer most commonly had to do with the excellence of its educational opportunities. These students have given us their confidence. We must be worthy of that confidence and supply them with a first-rate education that will prepare them as well as possible to cope with life in the last quarter of the twentieth century and the first quarter of the twenty-first.

Each brings his or her own set of talents and problems, concerns and aspirations. I believe that we offer the kind of intellectual, cultural, social, and athletic experiences that will allow each student to grow and mature at his or her own rate. In four years, if all goes well, they will leave, taking away skills and, I hope, wisdom.

Washington University's environment is conducive to learning—but of course learning in depth is difficult for young people, as well as for the rest of us. Distractions complicate matters, for rarely are the years between ages 17 and 22 completely tranquil. Self-motivation and self-reliance remain keys to success.

We expect a great deal of our students. Fortunately, they also expect much of themselves and, by and large, perform very well.

Our expectations for students could not be realized without top-notch faculty and adequate facilities. We are grateful to the many friends who, through their interest and support, help make possible the lively academic spirit of Washington University.

1975 This letter is written at the season of Thanksgiving. Traditionally, it is a letter sending holiday greetings, reporting on progress, and expressing appreciation. At Thanksgiving time 1975, with our worries about inflation, détente, inequities, and changing standards, it seems appropriate to consider a few of the things for which we can be especially thankful.

As Americans, we can be thankful for: a nation at peace; the vitality with which an idealistic people struggles with the inevitable limitations of human nature that confine us all, leaders and average citizens alike; the beauty of a land whose produce is sufficient to feed, clothe, and house its people; the resourcefulness and vigor of our citizenry; the tradition of freedom that underlies both our activity and our diversity, and gives meaning to individual lives.

We at Washington University can be thankful for our heritage of academic freedom and intellectual excellence, buildings that combine both beauty and function, tree-lined walks, well-stocked libraries, endowments from which we draw sustenance year after year; for our friends who accept us as we are, give encouragement when we are less than what we are striving to be, and at all times support us generously.

Finally, I am personally thankful for: the privilege of working at one of the nation's great universities; faculty colleagues who forever enlarge my vision and challenge my assumptions; administrators and staff without whose devoted service Washington University would quickly cease to function; the liveliness, optimism, idealism, and commitment of students who repeatedly renew my hope for humankind.

Even at Thanksgiving time, we know that all is far from perfect, yet we can be thankful for those farsighted individuals who are sensitive to what is still left undone and point to the tasks and challenges that confront us and our institutions. Especially, we can be thankful for the relentless quest for improvement that is so much a part of our tradition and culture.

1976 A person who has been away from a university campus for a while may feel a sense of estrangement. It may seem that, if one were to find the fountain of youth, return to age 18, and begin college again, the experience would be so alien and totally different from that of earlier eras as to be almost unrecognizable.

In a sense, such a fantasy touches on a truth. One does not have to look very far to note the marked changes in dress, hairstyle, or popular music that set apart the generations. One does not need to listen to much conversation to realize that a good deal of the subject matter was hardly in the public consciousness a generation ago. Only consider some of the phrases: "ecological crises," "affirmative action," "OPEC," "feminist movement," "TV-induced behavior."

Yet we can be so caught up in the process of change, especially on a university campus, that we miss the underlying continuities: the similarity of experience shared by each generation. Our hypothetical time traveler would find much that is familiar. Scholars and scientists, in their attempts to know and understand, are still grappling with their problems late at night and into the early morning hours, just as Arthur Holly Compton did in the 1920s or even Galileo in the early 1600s. The library, larger and better stocked, is still the centerpiece of the university, used by faculty and students alike to understand what has gone before and how our predecessors dealt with the difficulties and controversies of their day.

It would be evident to our friend that human factors are very much the same. Students are still faced with questions about their own lives: How shall I spend these years allotted to me? How shall I use my particular abilities in conformity with my hopes and my ethical principles? There is still the excitement of learning, of grasping new concepts, of testing one's own ideas against those of one's professors and classmates. There is still the same need to understand one's self and the world better. Our visitor would find the same idealism, the same ambition, the same hopes, the same despair from one's own days on campus. Sharing dreams and uncertainties with friends remains an essential part of the campus experience, as do fun and frolic.

Finally, our traveler would find that the institution is driven by the same convictions that drove our predecessors: that humankind can learn and profit from the analysis of experience, that knowledge and wisdom can be passed from generation to generation, that improving our understanding brings us closer to the truth, that we need not repeat over and over again the mistakes of the past. Without these hopes—without these convictions— the work of our University would be greatly diminished, and the institution would eventually fall into disuse.

We are deeply indebted to those who believe in Washington University and who share a sense of gratification in helping the University perform its mission well. Our task would be impossible if it were not for our friends who contribute in so many ways to our progress. This support is a wonderful expression of confidence in the quality and potential of our faculty and students. We accept it with appreciation and look forward to the coming months with enthusiasm.

1977 During much of the year, we in the modern world are deluged with numbers: Statistics indicate the success of a baseball player, measure the employment rates, assess the financial health of the nation, estimate the relative intelligence of today's students and even rank universities. We at Washington University are no different. Now, as 1977 ends, I should like to shift attention to the human qualities of the University. Numbers cannot express the spirit, the dedication, the sacrifice that have made us what we are, nor can they express the sense of excitement, fun, and accomplishment that are part and parcel of any college campus. I think it has always been so.

Washington University was built by people of vision and energy. As I walk around the campus, its beauty sinks in, and I muse about the achievements that have taken place in its buildings; however, I think also of the toil,

Arthur Holly Compton, who received a Nobel Prize in 1927, at work in his physics laboratory, c. 1931-1935

the sweat, the tears, and the treasure that have gone into making us what we are. At such times, I hope that we are living up to our obligations during these years for which we have responsibility.

From time to time, I try to figure out how our predecessors did it. I think there were at least three essentials: vision, teamwork, and confidence. They shared a grand dream that knowledge was better than ignorance, that humankind could be bettered by education. They did not feel they were building for themselves but for their fellow humans and those who would come after them. They worked together as a team, sharing the load, the responsibility, and the credit. They had confidence that they could influence the future—and they did.

Of course, the founders and leaders of Washington University did not succeed alone. For what we are today, we owe a debt to many people, among them talented, hardworking faculty and generous friends who shared the belief that a vital university is one of humankind's noble creations. We are grateful for this expression of confidence in our future. It is our inspiration for tomorrow.

1978 When I review the history of any successful institution, I am always struck by the persistent trials and recurring difficulties it has overcome. Since its founding 125 years ago, Washington University has survived wars, panics, and social unrest. It has been troubled by setbacks, disappointments, and irresolvable problems—yet it has progressed. So I am left to wonder: What were the qualities that enabled our predecessors to bring about this progress?

A basic ingredient, it seems to me, is faith. A positive relation to society requires trust and confidence in others. I suspect it has always been like that, but perhaps it is more so today. Many acts of faith are required. Unfortunately, faith must sometimes face disillusionment—perhaps as often as every month, every week, even every day—but without it our institutions would stagnate. Too much faith is better than too little. Success comes from starting fresh after each disappointment and never allowing oneself to become cynical, jaded, or untrusting.

A second basic ingredient is the appreciation of others. In any large endeavor, there are people with a wide array of skills and talents, with different perspectives and goals. To understand and appreciate this diversity, particularly when the goals of many are at variance with one's own hopes, calls for empathy and a great effort of will. The achievement of understanding, mutual trust, and appreciation is not only an end in itself, but it is also the prerequisite for major progress.

Fortunately for Washington University, those are qualities that, from early days to present, have helped our predecessors create an institution that is noble and lasting. We are grateful to those who have gone before. Without them, our institution would not today be one of the nation's great universities.

1979 I recently heard a story, probably apocryphal, about an official in the British Foreign Office who retired in the 1950s after a long and distinguished career. When asked about his major contribution, he replied that he had kept up people's spirits. Every year some diplomats and generals would predict the breakdown of world order and a terrible war. Every year he replied, "Nonsense. Everything will be all right. Don't worry." Then he added, "I was wrong only twice."

Most of us have trouble striking the right balance between optimism and pessimism. It is not easy to disentangle our assessments from those of people who surround us. Moods are highly contagious and undermine objectivity. We tend to be very much influenced by the most recent news, good or bad.

Sometimes there is a discrepancy between what we learn firsthand and what comes to us from others. For me, this discrepancy is apparent in higher education today. Most of what I see is good: bright and able students with youthful zeal and idealism, preparing themselves for important roles in our democracy; highly talented, creative faculty contributing to the knowledge and wisdom of the world and passing on what they know to succeeding generations; a public that generally understands, appreciates, and supports great universities. Much of what I read and hear secondhand, however, deals with trials, failures, and expected disasters.

In my set of balances, inflation probably plays too large a role. Nevertheless, here is my effort to strike a realistic balance.

- I am thankful for the intellectual, physical, and financial resources that allow Washington University to maintain an exciting academic community. I worry about the undermining effect of inflation on our capacity to do so.
- I am grateful for able, hardworking faculty who enlarge the minds of students and bring national and international honor to Washington University. I am deeply concerned that society is not recognizing this highly educated, intelligent group with appropriate economic and social rewards; faculty income is lagging not only behind inflation but also behind the income of other Americans. Genteel poverty is inappropriate for some of the nation's finest intellects.
- I take great satisfaction that so many of the brightest students come to Washington University, but I view with concern the advancing cost of higher education and the financial burden on families who want the best for their children.
- I am happy that our graduate and professional schools are the source of so many leaders in many walks of life. I regret that so often well-qualified applicants must be turned away.
- I enjoy the beauty of our campus: its inviting quadrangles and handsome buildings. I do not enjoy the high cost of maintenance and energy necessary to keep these buildings functional.
- I draw great satisfaction from the accomplishments of our students. I am concerned lest we forget that academic achievement is not the sole measure of success.

Professor James E. McLeod and his German class, September 1990

• I am pleased by the federal government's support of research and student financial aid, since the cost of these needs has outstripped the capacity of individual institutions. I deplore the increased intrusiveness of the federal bureaucracy, often with little understanding of the nature of education, and I am concerned that the creation of the new Department of Education will make matters worse instead of better.

I remain optimistic and hopeful. If anyone predicts disaster, I, like the British foreign officer, say, "Nonsense. Everything will be all right." I can also add, "Don't worry," because that is part of my job. I do not mind worrying for I believe in the importance of Washington University. Major universities are a vital part of our modern democratic nation. They are essential for supplying the coming generations with the technical and intellectual skills to run our complex society. Even more important, our graduates will be citizens in the world's leading democracy, charged with making difficult decisions that will affect the future of all humankind.

As we approach 1980, I can look to the future with renewed optimism that we will meet the challenges confronting us with the vision and dedication necessary for human betterment.

1980 I am composing this year-end letter soon after the national elections. It is a time of uncertainty as a new administration prepares its policies, and people are looking forward with concern as well as with hope. Higher education shares in the general problems of inflation and the crisis surrounding energy policy. In addition, our administrators and faculty members wonder how they will cope with the coming decline in the number of college-age young people.

Washington University is trying to plan intelligently for the future. Each school has been reviewing its challenges and aspirations and then testing these ideas against those of qualified outside persons, keeping our planning both as good and as realistic as possible. The process has been—and should continue to be—helpful.

It is impossible to do justice to all the excellent ideas that surface in such a review, but let me attempt a very brief description of how we see Washington University's mission. Washington University is one of the nation's approximately 50 to 60 "research universities." These institutions have a self-imposed obligation not only to teach well but also to encourage faculty in scholarly and scientific research and in artistic endeavors.

About half of the nation's major research institutions are independent and the other half are public. Washington University and the other research universities educate many of the country's brightest young people. Most of the nation's basic research is carried out by these faculties, and a large percentage of the strong doctoral programs exist on these campuses. From them graduate a disproportionate share of America's scholars, scientists, and leaders. At best, both the faculty and students form a community of learners.

Washington University should continue to play an important role in this group. We are the only such institution in our region. More importantly, we are helping to ensure that America will have as its greatest asset a well-educated, technically able, flexible citizenry—people of great competence who are wise enough to provide leadership to a modern democracy. It is our job to attract young people of high potential and to give them the best possible education for the roles they will play. In addition, it is from Washington University that new ideas and concepts will come that will allow our nation to change and adapt.

However, if we looked only to the future, we would become unmoored. Faculty also preserve experiences and works of the past, supplying the perspectives that we hope will help America proceed in an intelligent way, linked through historic memory to the best of our heritage.

Of course, I would not limit the potential benefits of scholarship and research to our nation alone. The books and articles the faculty write travel the globe. The concepts developed in the laboratories and in the clinics cross national boundaries. The ideas will be considered and pondered by the Russians, Poles, Chinese, and French, and in time adopted for the good of them and their children as well as for the good of our people and our own children.

An investment in Washington University, whether it be the life's work of a dedicated faculty member or the resources of an individual or corporation, is an investment in the future. Americans have always been a forward-looking people. Even in a time of uncertainty and high inflation, Washington University should be able to continue to give outstanding service to the nation. I believe that, given the complexities of the times, the University will be needed more than ever.

Washington University does not succeed alone, of course. Support from the community, from foundations and companies, from alumni and friends across the country, contributes importantly to our ability to build quality in higher education and speed progress in scientific research. We deeply appreciate this expression of faith.

1981 Each year around Thanksgiving I write to express appreciation to the many friends who make Washington University possible. Especially, I want to thank those who have been so helpful to the University and to me personally since I became Chancellor a decade ago.

Ten years is a long time to be a university chancellor or president. I have evolved from being a newcomer to being a senior chief officer of a major university. Ten years is also enough time to gain some perspectives, one of which I have been thinking about lately.

I am struck by how rapidly our interests and moods change. Amazingly, all college campuses in the United States and, indeed, in the western world seem to shift together in synchronous fashion, as if coordinated by some unseen conductor. We can scarcely begin to understand how all this happens.

What we do know is that our best seers often totally miss the dominant trend that may be only a year or two in the future. Ten years ago, many predictions were made about the coming decade. Today, much of what was written seems hopelessly dated, if not seriously misguided. The authors succumbed to the obviously still-present temptation to extrapolate the future from the experience of the immediate past, not taking into account longer-range rhythms or the possibility of dramatic shifts in direction.

As a result, we are apt to be caught off guard more often than we should be. Sudden changes can bring to us success if we are positioned well— or agony if we are not. At the moment, for example, we at Washington University and the families of our students are adapting to the major governmental effort to place more responsibility on the individual and on the private sector.

It is important that each successive challenge be met, that each alternating national mood be taken into account. Yet it is easy to become too enthralled by the last change or by the gestalt of the moment and then to run the risk of shortchanging those less-glamorous elements on which the University is built, and which endure from generation to generation. I am thinking, of course, of such things as:

- the need of our great democracy for broadly educated leaders;
- the dependence of the modern world on well-trained professionals;
- the opportunity to satisfy the inner drive of many young people to learn and understand;
- the importance of a community of scholars who preserve the experiences of the past and think through the problems of the present, both scientific and cultural.

Thanksgiving 1981 is an appropriate time to express profound appreciation to all who helped us meet immediate challenges and, even more important, continue to work on our basic responsibilities.

1982 "Almost everything can be better understood by a knowledge of what preceded it. As long as there are men and women who are interested in their own world, there will be those who will be curious about how it came to be."

The above quote was taken from a manuscript on Marcus Aurelius written by George E. Kassabaum: a graduate of Washington University, a faculty member, a Board member, a gifted architect, and a co-founder of HOK, Inc., who died this summer at age 61. George was interested in Marcus Aurelius because he wondered how the Romans had achieved a sense of public responsibility that underlay a stable world order lasting for many centuries. He was especially drawn to Stoics like Marcus Aurelius, for, as he wrote:

> "This group believed it was wrong to consider a position of leadership as a thing merely to gratify personal ambition. The leader's interest should be for the good of the state."

George went on to show how the stoic way of life could affect one:

> "Hour by hour, resolve to do the task of the hour, carefully, with unaffected dignity, affectionately, freely, and justly. You can avoid all distractions that might interfere with such performance if every act is done as though it were the last act of your life. Free yourself from random aims and curb any tendency to let the passions of emotion, hypocrisy, self-love, and dissatisfaction with your allotted share cause you to ignore the commands of reason.

> "...Neither yesterday nor the day before was perfect, so, realistically, why should you expect today to be?"

One passage from his manuscript helped me to put George Kassabaum's untimely death in perspective:

George E. Kassabaum, BArch '47, February 1978

1982

"What is it to die? If you look solely at the nature of death itself and with the analysis of reason strip it of its phantom terrors which our imagination assigns, then you will see that death is only a process of nature that is essential to our well-being—an operation of a force that is benevolent to other things—and none but a child could be terrified at that."

Thanksgiving 1982 is a time to be grateful for the lives and endeavors of all those who, like George Kassabaum, work toward the improvement of our society and use positions of power, leadership, and trust for the common good and not for the gratification of personal ambition.

Washington University could not exist without such men and women. For almost 130 years their efforts on behalf of the University have contributed to its progress. I deeply appreciate the steadfast help we have so regularly received.

1983 Thanksgiving is my annual opportunity to thank those who have done so much to make Washington University possible. This year, with the ALLIANCE FOR WASHINGTON UNIVERSITY successfully under way, there is so much to be thankful for that I scarcely know where to begin.

I believe I am most especially thankful for the generosity of spirit that characterizes so many individuals. That human beings are cooperative, altruistic, and generous is no surprise. Our species would not have survived the Stone Age without those traits. It seems to me that what is special today is the enthusiasm with which so many people join together to support the institutions and organizations that embody the ideals and hopes of our society. Modern life makes it difficult to be effective on one's own or even with a few people. To further great causes, it is usually necessary to work together with others, many of whom one does not even know personally. Fortunately, we find within ourselves not only the capacity to join in, but also joy and satisfaction in doing so.

W.L. Hadley Griffin, LLB '47, chairman of the Board of Trustees, Chancellor William H. Danforth, and George H. Capps, AB '39, JD '39, general chairman of the ALLIANCE FOR WASHINGTON UNIVERSITY, with findings from the Commission on the Future of Washington University, 1981

1983

Is it overly optimistic to think that all the effort and all the treasure poured by altruistic individuals into Washington University and other institutions will make a measurable difference and will lead in the long run to a better, more civilized society? I believe that our efforts make a difference; and I have never thought of myself as an optimist, but rather as a realist. In the introduction to his book, *Pluto's Republic*, Peter Medawar found an even better way of stating the point:

> "[My words] may give the impression that I am an 'optimist,' but indeed I am no such thing. I prefer to describe myself as a 'meliorist'— one who believes that the world can be improved by finding out what is wrong with it and then taking steps to put it right."

This year, I give special thanks for meliorists with generous and altruistic temperaments. Theirs is an enabling spirit that helps our independent universities fulfill their responsibilities and forge sound plans for the future.

1984 Thanksgiving is, of course, a national celebration. We in the United States have countless blessings: peace in a dangerous world; an economy strong enough to feed, clothe, and house us all; traditions of freedom and personal liberty; a heritage of successful struggle to bring together diverse people in harmony and justice. We have much for which to be thankful.

Closer to home, I am thankful for the magnificent generosity of our friends. This generosity has brought us to the two-thirds mark in our ALLIANCE FOR WASHINGTON UNIVERSITY campaign, adding 11 professorships, 50 new endowed scholarship funds, and three important buildings on our campuses. Even I, with long experience in the generosity of the larger Washington University family, have been surprised by this outpouring of support and confidence. My spirit is buoyed by the faith that we shall reach our goal.

I am also thankful that, with you and many others, I can play a small part in keeping intact the great human chain that preserves the learning of our species and recreates civilization anew for every generation. This chain extends back to antiquity and forward into the future—I hope forever. For the last eight centuries, universities have played a central role in this process and will continue to do so as far into the future as I can see. It is a privilege as well as a responsibility to be part of this historic adventure.

1985 This year, in the midst of the $300 million ALLIANCE FOR WASHINGTON UNIVERSITY, I have more reason than ever to be grateful. I expected the generosity of the University family to continue, but I have been overwhelmed. The outpouring of support indicates a confidence in education and in Washington University that humbles me. We will work even harder to justify your faith.

People ask me occasionally, "When will this striving and sacrifice end?" I imagine the same question was asked of William Greenleaf Eliot when Washington University was created, and of Robert S. Brookings when he moved the University to our Hilltop Campus and rebuilt the School of Medicine. I am certain the question was asked of Ethan Shepley in the 1950s when the University constructed the dormitories and the John M. Olin Library in order to become a national institution.

Fortunately, there is work left to do. The opportunities forever outstrip the resources; the challenges never end. Each generation—even each decade—brings new challenges that must be met and surmounted to keep faith with the past and renew the search for excellence.

This excellence is never attained once and for all. In a university, excellence is a constant search for deeper understandings, for clearer explanations, for better predictability, for more profound art. Excellence means the passing to oncoming generations, not just of subject matter, but also

*Robert S. Brookings at his desk in Cecilwood, today
known as Alumni House,* c. 1911-1923

of restless strivings to be better. Excellence is a state of mind, not a resting place. What Toynbee said of civilization applies:

"It is a movement and not a condition, a voyage and not a harbor."

To all who help us keep alive the striving for excellence, and especially to members of the Board whose extra measure of assistance is bringing our goal within reach, I offer my special gratitude this Thanksgiving.

1986 The year 1986 has been special. As the result of the efforts of hundreds of volunteers and the generosity of more than 53,000 donors, the ALLIANCE FOR WASHINGTON UNIVERSITY reached the $300 million mark 18 months ahead of schedule. Shortly thereafter, the Danforth Foundation and the Spencer T. and Ann W. Olin Foundation added marvelous extra support that will bring great benefits in the decades ahead. I could not be more grateful to all the donors and volunteers. I am thankful also to the faculty, students, and administrators whose day-to-day dedication and hard work make Washington University a vital intellectual community, able to inspire confidence in you and the many others who have contributed so much.

Taking a step back, one can see that our ALLIANCE is part of the great American tradition of voluntary action so built into our national life that we sometimes forget it is unique in the history of the world. In 1835, Alexis de Tocqueville was struck by this characteristic:

"Suppose that an [American]...thinks of some enterprise, and that enterprise has a direct bearing on the welfare of society; it does not come into his head to appeal to public authority for its help. He publishes his plan, offers to carry it out, summons other individuals to aid his efforts, and personally struggles against all obstacles. No doubt he is often less successful than the state would have been in his place, but in the long run the sum of all private undertakings far surpasses anything the government might have done."

From the voluntary associations described by de Tocqueville have come the independent institutions, free of government control, that have added so much to the strength and vitality of American life. In 1835, it could not have seemed possible that this characteristic could survive in a geographically much larger, more densely packed nation of more than 241 million people. Nor could one have imagined effective voluntarism as the support required by private institutions grew so large that many of those working for the same cause might not know the names or faces of many of their co-workers.

Happily, we have had the privilege of helping to write a new chapter in the history of American voluntarism showing that democratic pluralism is alive and well in the 1980s. Together, we have helped to demonstrate that independent institutions can prosper in the modern era on a scale large enough to be of significance nationally and internationally. I hope you share my satisfaction in being part of this accomplishment.

As always, new strength brings new opportunities and new responsibilities. I am confident that our striving will not cease as we attempt to be worthy of the hard work and treasure that has brought us this far.

1987 In this annual Thanksgiving letter, I should like to express special thanks for the generosity of spirit and for the continuity of effort that were so evident in 1987.

An institution, like a human being, usually defines its character not from one momentous happening, but rather from the cumulative effect of thousands of decisions made day after day, week after week, year after year. If these

Scientists and Nobel Prize winners Gerty T. and Carl F. Cori in their Washington University School of Medicine laboratory, 1947

decisions are shaped by a coherent set of principles, the institution develops a character that people can understand and to which they will respond.

As I read the history of Washington University, for nearly a century we have held the vision of having here in St. Louis one of the world's greatest universities. Such a grand vision cannot be transformed into reality overnight, nor can one ever point to a single year as marking a transition. Nonetheless, a number of happenings in the academic year 1986-87 gave evidence of progress. Recognition came repeatedly to faculty, including two Nobel prizes for work started at Washington University. Students did well, with awards coming to the Math Team and to *Student Life*. The ALLIANCE FOR WASHINGTON UNIVERSITY achieved the highest total ever for an American university in a single development campaign. The endowment, which might be thought of as our gift to the future, moved up in size to ninth in the nation. In addition, the reputation of our institution has grown, as evidenced by an increase of 22.3 per cent in applications for this fall's freshman undergraduate class.

None of these things could have happened without a series of excellent decisions dating back to the time after World War II when Arthur Holly Compton became chancellor. If we look more deeply, the roots of our success go back into the nineteenth century.

We are fortunate in our heritage, but that heritage will mean little unless we use it well in our era and build on it for those who come after. Thus, I am especially grateful to those with whom I have the privilege of working, for I believe that we are using our heritage well. I am certain that we will hand on to those who come after us a Washington University with its strengths and traditions elaborated and enhanced, ready for each new faculty member and for each freshman student.

1988 My grandchildren frequently interrupt the writing of this annual Thanksgiving letter. When grandchildren are around, who could not be thankful for the goodness of life? I hope, therefore, that you may forgive a personal note in the letter.

Frequently, I am asked what I actually do as Chancellor. Sometimes I wonder myself. In one of my favorite stories, my youngest daughter explains to a friend that Daddy does not do anything. "He used to be a doctor and make people well, but now he just goes to meetings."

Actually, I can no longer view myself as a physician, although that calling of my younger years will always shape my view of the world. Despite all of the advances in care, I still feel at home with doctors and in that special culture of those who have the responsibility for the life and health of others.

I am no longer a scientist, although the thrill of trying to understand a small segment of reality and then generalize from those findings will never leave me. Always, I will honor those who add to human understanding. I consider them to be the hope of our world.

I can hardly consider myself an educator. The real learning at the University occurs in the classrooms, the libraries, and the laboratories under the guidance of scholars/teachers who devote their lives to this great endeavor. Only look to China to see what happens when the education of a generation is disrupted.

I am an academic administrator. I believe in administration. Without people who see to it that things run well, any institution would be in shambles. The creativity, perseverance, and energy of my administrative colleagues have contributed more to Washington University than I can ever put into words. They are especially important because my own skills are limited—the product of on-the-job learning.

I like to think that my present vocation is to help preserve and build an institution that embodies values and promotes activities in which I believe. Each year, institutions seem more important to me. Of necessity, it seems, we humans arrange ourselves into groups. Americans especially are devoted

William H. Danforth with his youngest daughter, Elizabeth ("Beth"), age 5, 1967

to organizing. The richness and variety of our national life comes in great part from the many institutions that we create: colleges and universities; schools and businesses; religious, political, and social groups; organizations to disseminate information and opinion; societies for human betterment; and on and on and on.

These institutions amplify individual efforts and give permanence to our ideals and dreams so that they will endure beyond our own brief lives. Our institutions offer us support when we express ourselves in word and action. They are buffers against those with greater political, economic, or social power. They offer us personal boons, such as the comradeship of working side by side with others who share visions that we hold dear.

Washington University does all these things. At its heart, our institution is a community of scholars who add to the world's store of knowledge and wisdom, and provide education for some of the most promising of coming generations. This community started long before we were born and will be here long after we leave the earth. We are all part of an institution with a heritage of striving for excellence, an institution that never ages, but rather is constantly renewed so as always to be ready for each new faculty member and each new freshman. What could be a greater privilege?

I am fortunate to be engaged in this project with a large company whom I respect and enjoy. This Thanksgiving, I give thanks for Washington University and, especially, for friends, alumni, faculty, students, and staff, who are my co-workers in this great enterprise and who make our common task a joy, as well as a success.

1989 This annual Thanksgiving letter is the result of thinking about last summer's trip to the Soviet Union. It is exciting to visit a country engaged in a massive attempt to "restructure" an entire multicultural, multiethnic nation. A major goal is to catch up with and surpass the West economically:

just as Peter the Great tried to catch up with and surpass the West militarily; just as Catherine the Great tried to do so architecturally; just as Stalin and later Russian leaders tried with a different approach to do so economically, technically, and militarily.

It is, of course, too soon to judge the results. Eventually, our grand-children will read in history books about the extent of Mr. Gorbachev's success—and even whether or not he survived politically. During the trip, I tried to understand as much as I could but, as usual, I learned as much about myself and my own country as about the country I was visiting.

I came away struck especially by the many things for which we in our nation can give thanks. For example:

- Our ability to seek the truth and report it as we find it. We have no official history that distorts our past for political purposes. Rather, our history is constantly open to new information, to reinterpretation, and to argument, in a continuing effort to understand who we really are and why.
- Our tradition of liberal education for a democratic society. This educa-tion aims to produce a broadly informed leadership with the potential for understanding the context of their work and for taking part effec-tively in the decision making of a democratic society.
- Our variety of institutions—profit, non-profit, governmental, non-gov-ernmental, and quasi-governmental—led by able persons experienced in making decisions and living with the results. These institutions, so essen-tial to a decentralized society, have been created over generations. They cannot be reproduced overnight.
- Our traditions of change and reform in politics, business, education, the arts—in fact, all walks of life. Change in the United States usually wells up from the people, often catching the leaders by surprise, rather than as in the Soviet Union being centrally directed from the political lead-ership. All societies need constant reform. We can and do reform ours institution by institution, sector by sector, instead of having to address

everything at once. We have the opportunity to change constantly and steadily rather than in convulsive bursts.

- Our opportunity and our responsibility to lead the world in the creation of a successful multiethnic, multiracial society. We have a history of progress; we have political traditions emphasizing justice and human rights; we have educational and economic resources; and, most of all, we have the vision to evolve an ever more enlightened, just, and productive society with opportunities for all. No other nation has so great an opportunity as we do. It is a wonderful challenge; such challenges give meaning to life.

Closer to home, I am thankful for another successful year at Washington University. I am thankful for the opportunity to serve one of the nation's institutions that contributes mightily to the traditions of freedom, to an educated citizenry, and to the stream of knowledge so necessary to the continuing success of our nation.

1990 This annual Thanksgiving letter will focus on Washington University's international links. This fall, more than 800 foreign nationals from 70 countries are studying with us. Most will sooner or later return to their homelands; some will remain in the U.S. permanently. These individuals add interest, vitality, and an opportunity for all of us to learn from them.

This summer I, along with a small group, visited with Washington University alumni, students, and parents in seven Asian cities: Seoul, Tokyo, Taipei, Hong Kong, Bangkok, Kuala Lumpur, and Singapore. In each city, we were received with warmth and gracious hospitality by people deeply interested in maintaining ties and increasing contacts with Washington University. It was a pleasure to see old friends and make new ones.

The accomplishments of our alumni are impressive. Quite a few fellow

William K.Y. Tao, MSME '50, emeritus trustee and retired president, BSC, Inc., 1977

academics have attained considerable distinction. The president of the new Hong Kong University of Science and Technology, the most recent past president of Korea University, and the dean of the Graduate School of Business Administration at Yonsei University in Korea all have degrees from Washington University. So do many successful business people who are heading important organizations and successful enterprises. We met quite a few architects, including internationally famous Fumihiko Maki of Tokyo.

Some of our graduates are engaged in large architectural projects that are changing the face of important cities along the Pacific rim. Physicians with Washington University ties have made and are making major contributions to practice, education, and science. We met artists of distinction and talked with social workers who are ministering with skill and dedication.

The stream of young people from other nations coming to the United States for study continues to grow. Fortunately, the path can be traveled both ways. Increasingly, young Americans realize the importance of learning about and visiting other cultures. This semester, more than 1,600 Washington undergraduates will be enrolled in foreign language courses. Approximately 260 are abroad for part of their education. About 20 of this last group will be engaged in internships in European businesses.

We Americans have a long way to go in learning as much about foreign cultures as others know about ours, but a start has been made and Washington University, thanks to the diligent work of many members of the faculty, is doing its part.

I view all of this exchange as very good. It is evidence that American higher education is recognized as the best in the world. Some worry that we are, in effect, "educating our economic competition." We probably are, but since the end of World War II our national policy has been to help other countries strengthen their economies on the theory that by so doing we foster world peace, stability, and well being. Moreover, even if we tried, we could not put fences around ideas. Sooner or later—mostly sooner—they would escape. No modern nation has created a successful society based on secrecy. Any lack of openness of American universities would soon lead the ablest students from all over the world to seek education elsewhere. The result would likely be that the mantle of leadership in higher education would pass somewhere else, and American influence would fade.

In my view, we should do all we can to encourage young Americans to learn about and from other cultures and other peoples. Only in this way can we continue our economic successes and our tradition of world leadership.

At this time of the year, I give special thanks for the role of Washington University in educating young people from around the globe and in educating young Americans for the modern world.

1991 This year, my Thanksgiving letter will be a little longer than usual, for I should like to comment on the contrast between what I experience on the Washington University campus and what I learn about American higher education from the press and from television.

It helps to go back to the end of World War II, when it became evident that improvements in the health of Americans and the economic growth of the nation would depend on scientific discoveries. Since only the federal government was in a position to finance work that does not have a rapid payoff, it was decided that the nation's basic science would be performed in universities. Not all countries followed the same course; for example, most German research is performed in special institutes. The results from American research have been spectacular. The practical benefits include the polio vaccine, modern agriculture, advanced computers, lasers, antibiotics, and modern communications. According to Frank Press, the president of the National Academy of Sciences, the list of emerging technologies, mostly growing out of science, is projected to account for a trillion dollars in new business by the end of the decade.

*Washington University student with participant in
the Special Olympics,* February 1991

1991

During this period, American universities have increased in strength and prestige. Young people now journey from all over the world to be educated in the United States. They come because of the quality of the faculty, because of the individual attention, and because of the freedom they have to learn, grow, and change. Other nations have tried—and continue to try—to create similar institutions, but to do so is difficult, because no other country has given faculty and students so much freedom to teach and to learn or their institutions so much freedom to create themselves and chart their own destinies.

So far what I have described sounds like paradise, but one has only to pick up a newspaper or to turn on one's television set to learn that universities are beset by troubles, many of their own making. One might conclude that university-based research is tainted with fraud; that university leaders are ripping off the taxpayers for yachts and parties; that most research is trivial and never cited anyway; that research is subverting the teaching mission; that colleges and universities are overcharging and then providing teachers who do not speak English; that college education is not worth the investment; that free speech no longer graces American campuses; that universities engage in pork-barrel politics; that enforcement of drug laws is lax or nonexistent on college campuses; that cheating is rampant; that affirmative action programs are of questionable morality and even legality; and that athletics are worse.

What is going on? How can we understand what we read and hear? What should we do?

In one sense, we have seen such criticism before. Town-gown disputes are as old as universities. They are inherent in the ever-present misunderstandings between the young and the less-than-young, between the critic and the activist, between intellectuals and people of affairs. Today, the town no longer stops at the city limits but has become the nation or even the world, bound together by an increasingly effective communications system. Every problem and every bizarre human action is highlighted. Despite the best will in the world, it is difficult not to generalize from anecdotal reports and conclude that there is something inherently wrong with the entire university system that should and must be fixed.

What I experience firsthand, however, continues to lift my spirits. I see students—as idealistic and bright as ever—learning, growing, and maturing in a complex and difficult world, many giving voluntary service to the elderly, to the disabled, to the poor. I see the young successfully wrestling to understand each other across racial and cultural gulfs. I talk with parents who have sacrificed to give their children a Washington University education and are thrilled with the results. I note the increased internationalism of our campus, young people from all over the world coming to learn and, increasingly, our students going off to Europe, to Asia, to Africa, to South and Central America, in order to study and to work. Faculty are working on curricular development, better methods of teaching, and new technology for the classroom. I rejoice with professors recognized nationally and internationally for advances in knowledge and in understanding. I see junior faculty of great promise beginning their careers at Washington University and senior faculty completing careers of service to students and to scholarship.

The great issues are debated, as they should be; I could never even imagine suppression of free speech at Washington University. I am privileged to associate with able and dedicated staff who arrive early in the morning and work until late in the evening. I talk with senior students and alumni who report that Washington University was one of the most rewarding and important experiences in their lives. I spend time with marvelous friends who share with us their time and treasure to make Washington University possible because they have faith that young people can learn and that each generation can be better than the last. I could never become jaded or discouraged about our University.

Do I think Washington University is perfect in an otherwise imperfect world? Of course not. I sometimes think that every complaint anyone could possibly make comes to the Chancellor's Office. It is just that I do not expect human affairs ever to work out perfectly; I believe that the imperfections of higher education are small compared with the accomplishments. We all know there is always much to criticize and improve. The important challenge is to get on with trying to better ourselves and our institutions.

Am I being blind and, carried away by our successes, have I overlooked our shortcomings and failures? I don't think so. Rather, I think that this kind of public criticism and generalizing from a few incidents has become a way of life in late-twentieth-century America. I don't like it; it is unpleasant, but it is not all bad. Intense criticism, even that which unfairly damages individuals and institutions, is a better way to change things than the suppression of criticism and change followed by cataclysmic upheavals characteristic of dictatorships of the right or the left. Criticism is one of the ways we in our democratic society cleanse ourselves.

Finally, we all have to deal with our problems lest they destroy us, but we cannot allow a few bad—even very bad—experiences to corrode our enterprise or our nation with suspicion and cynicism. The marvelous past and the promising future of American higher education are too great.

Our primary responsibilities as academics remain to learn and to teach, to add to the sum of human understanding and to pass on to the coming generations both what we know and our enthusiasm for the search. With your help, Washington University will continue to grow in service to our students, to the community, and to the world.

1992 This year, I am preparing my Thanksgiving letter during the 1992 political campaigns. The dominant mood of the body politic seems sour. Political entities are losing legitimacy in many countries, including our own; long-accepted social customs are being altered and sometimes abandoned; the economy is uncertain. There is plenty to worry about. And to top it all off, the negative political advertising would make one believe that no one in the world is to be trusted.

Thanksgiving is different. It carries a message of gratitude. Thanksgiving is the time to count not our grievances, but our blessings. When we do, we find there are blessings in abundance. What would the early Pilgrims think of air-conditioning, central heating, and blueberries in the winter? What would they think of modern medicine and sanitation, or young mothers who expect to see each of their children grow to adulthood, or so many elderly people living active lives? They would marvel at travel to Europe or Asia in less than 24 hours or access to a world of information just by going to the library or turning on the television. They might note that today our children are not conscripted and sent off to battle as they were in some European countries in which they had lived. They might admire our efforts to protect the rights of children, women, minorities, and the disabled. They would certainly conclude that we humans, despite our ever-present problems, live in an earthly paradise. Of course, disappointment, hardship, suffering, and death are with us always. As Buddha said, "Disease is not the cause of death. Birth is." But even suffering and death can often be delayed and made more tolerable by modern medicine. The inevitable concomitants of life should not blind us to the great blessings of the modern age.

Why then is the electorate so sour? Perhaps what tempts us to complain is a fantasy of a utopian world imagined from television or a novel in which everyone is lovable, where all problems are easily solvable, where hardship and suffering happen only to other people. Compared to that, our world may seem dismal and tawdry, but compared to the realities of other times and places we can indeed count our blessings as we celebrate Thanksgiving.

Among the blessings I count is Washington University, a venerable but ever-young institution dedicated to the preservation, transmission, and enhancement of knowledge and wisdom; with its great traditions intact. I also count as blessings our many friends and supporters whose vision and generosity make possible such an institution.

June 1993 Some have asked if I might write more "Thanksgiving-type" letters about matters of interest at Washington University and beyond. I shall try several a year, although I want neither to wear out my welcome nor to write without something to say.

This letter grows out of talks with some of you about the national debates concerning curricula. To gain perspective, it is helpful to think about Commencement, which marks the completion of a course of study.

On May 14, the Class of 1993 will graduate wearing gowns that were fashionable in the late Middle Ages. They will be thinking of the present and the future. Marching ahead of them in the procession will be the Class of 1943, attending their fiftieth reunion and likely thinking of the present and the past. The question is: What kind of education would best have prepared the Class of 1943 for the next 50 years?

The Class of 1943, born about 1921, probably average 72 years in age. In their early years, economic times were good. Then when they were about nine, the Great Depression hit. They were 18 when Hitler invaded Poland and 20 at the time of Pearl Harbor. Most of the young men went to war, and some were among the 407,000 Americans who never returned. To put that in its larger context, they were among the 35 to 60 million people who died in that most terrible of all wars.

Born in the time of silent films and the Model T Ford, the members of the Class of 1943 have ridden in jet airplanes, watched cable television, and seen men walk on the moon. Nuclear power has been unleashed, and the Soviet Union has risen and fallen. They have moved from the industrial to the information age.

The members of the Class of 1943 have participated in the American success story, creating the most productive economy ever seen. They have watched it spread around the globe. Life has been richer, freer of disease, and more varied than at any time in human history. Never have people lived so well or so long. Free societies have been vindicated; in fact, people of many nations long for democracy and freedom. Their generation may

Washington University students, all members of the Enlisted Reserve Corps, 1943

be the most successful the world has ever seen. Yet all has not been free of strain and unease. Some have been nearly disoriented by changes in music and language and, more importantly, by changes in moral perception. Family life is different and less certain. All over the world, children are suffering, deprived, ill, malnourished. A recent study showed that only 10 per cent of the children in Rumania are healthy. Even in our country, children are bearing much of this nation's burden of poverty, lack of family stability, community upheavals, and poor education.

Great success does not mean we have reached the Garden of Eden. Humans never have and undoubtedly never will.

The subject of this letter is education, not world affairs, but there is a relation between the two. What education would best have prepared the Class of 1943 for the world in which they have lived? There are no easy answers, but here are a few ideas that have come up in discussions with individuals who lived through those changes:

- Proficiency in English, reading, writing, and speaking
- Knowledge of a foreign language and foreign culture
- Ability to handle numbers
- Understanding of history
- Insight into science and how science works
- Understanding of individual and group behavior through the humanities and the social sciences
- Education appropriate to one's profession

It would have been more important to learn the basics, which are unlikely to change rapidly, than the frills. Learning how to learn and how to evaluate new knowledge would have been essential, as would learning about moral and ethical values, and the kinds of difficult choices that all humans must make. Perhaps the greatest gift a faculty member could have passed on was the fun and excitement of learning and of the intellectual endeavor.

We cannot go back and redo the education of the 1940s, but perhaps we can draw on the experience of the lives of the Class of 1943, and the relevance of education to those lives, to put some of the current debates into perspective.

$\backsim$

August 1993 This letter is another effort to write several "Thanksgiving-type" letters a year. My June letter described the enormous changes in society since the graduation of the Class of 1943 fifty years ago. I said:

> "The members of the Class of 1943 have participated in the American success story, creating the most productive economy ever seen. They have watched it spread around the globe. Life has been richer, freer of disease, and more varied than at any time in human history. Never have people lived so well or so long. Free societies have been vindicated..."

The question is: How do the extraordinary successes of those now in their 70s relate to the challenges facing the Class of 1993, now in their 20s? Of course, this question is not new. Every human success is followed by new challenges and new problems. Growth in population follows improved agriculture. Rapid transportation spreads infectious diseases. The conquest of childhood illnesses allows more individuals to live to the age of Alzheimer's disease. A stronger economy increases the rate of depletion of natural resources and adds to pollution. Those engaged in solving the problems of the day seldom foresee the unintended consequences that success will surely bring. What they do realize is that if they fail, if their challenges overwhelm them, disaster will certainly follow.

Our commencement speaker, Dr. Peter H. Raven, director of the Missouri Botanical Garden, clearly outlined some of today's challenges. He said, in part:

Washington University faculty members Mona Van Duyn, later poet laureate from 1992 to 1993, and her husband Jarvis Thurston, 1975

August 1993

"Over the past 40 years, we've lost a fifth of the world's topsoil, destroyed a significant fraction of the ozone layer, set the world on a course toward significantly warmer temperatures...cut down a third of the world's forests...put millions of species...at risk...consuming as a human race 40 per cent of everything that the world produces, with our population still rising.

"We Americans...have opportunities that are limited only by our imaginations, but...we have to stop acting...as if we are sleepwalking....we must think and act as pioneers....The world is one and the sustainable resources of our common planetary home are limited."

No human success can ever be final. The generation of the Class of 1943 has left the Class of 1993 great boons and marvelous opportunities, but not Utopia. No matter what the success of those who have gone before, each new generation must muster courage and creativity to meet its special challenges.

Because we can never go back to a simpler age or even slow the rate of change, our civilization seems to be on a perpetual escalator bringing us to ever-greater opportunities and ever more complex challenges. Of course, preparing students for an evolving world is the job of universities. Our task is to enhance learning and to improve and extend education so that each generation will be as ready as possible for the challenges that will surely come.

My final charge to the Class of 1993 included the following:

"Keep alive hope and good will. Pay attention to the good before the evil. Put your trust in your fellow human beings and in your common future."

All of us on this planet have a common future. We have no choice but to put our trust in others of our species in the hope that our successors, like our predecessors, can build on past accomplishments to create new solutions and new opportunities for their children and grandchildren.

November 1993 Thanksgiving 1993 is again a time to count our blessings. Hope is high, with new opportunities for peace in the Middle East. This letter, however, will focus on the response of this community to a disaster close to home.

The Flood of '93 has dominated the news about St. Louis. The Mississippi and Missouri Rivers rose inexorably for 79 days. The waters overtopped and undermined levees, flowed over 10,240 acres of farmland, drove 55,000 families in the upper-Midwest region from their homes, and did $15 to $20 billion worth of damage to farms, homes, and businesses. The Army Corps of Engineers and private citizens had labored for decades to confine the river. Levees and flood walls, erected with vast sums of money, kept some cities and villages dry, but in doing so narrowed the river channel—thereby raising the water level and bringing more devastation to less well-protected areas.

We learned again that Nature is unpredictable and untamable and that good works sometimes have unintended, adverse consequences.

How the river is best controlled is a question that will be debated for decades. The resultant policies will be tested the next time the waters rise. There is an old saying: "How do you avoid mistakes?" "By experience." "How do you get experience?" "By learning from your mistakes."

The human response was inspiring. Thousands volunteered to fill and stack sandbags, to serve in shelters, to pack and load relief supplies, to interview flood victims, and so on and on. The helping spirit was not limited to Midwestern neighbors. A group of firemen from Delaware took their vacation time to come to Missouri just to help. The Red Cross, the Salvation Army, and government officials at all levels worked effectively. Individuals and corporations donated generously to flood relief.

Many from Washington University took part. The faculty and students of the George Warren Brown School of Social Work lent their skills. The Washington University Medical Center made 50 apartments available if needed for displaced families. Most students were away during the worst of

To Whom It May Concern; 10-4-93

On a Saturday in August after the Great Flood of '93 hit Mom's house, we were blessed with 10 fantastic volunteers from your school. They had the worse jo... ...imagine (shelving ... ...ud from the base... ...the yard).

They ... until the end and ... workers. They sho... ...in later lif... ...didn't leave a... ...me to us. The... ...will tell the...

We ... ay ours and over ... grateful we are to each of them. We were as interested too in them as they as to where the water had reached, etc.

Washington University freshman Kati Gardos, AB '97, helping to clean up flooded homes, 1993

November 1993

the flood, but over Labor Day weekend alone some 200 student volunteers worked to help with the aftermath. Other students organized warehouses of donated goods, answered hotlines, and put on fund-raising events.

A group headed by Vice Provost Harry Kisker continues to monitor the needs and community response so as to advise faculty, staff, and students how they can be most helpful in the cleanup and to people struggling to regain a normal life. The response of the community, including Washington University people, has been magnificent. The flood has shown the human spirit at its best. The enclosed letter describes the response of one family to our students.

Last September, when we thought the crisis had passed, rains caused further flooding of the Meramec, Missouri, Mississippi, Cuivre, Illinois, Kaskaskia, Bourbeuse, and Big rivers. Students responded by sandbagging in Valley Park, Festus, and Chesterfield.

The job of cleaning up and of returning to normal life will last for months or even years. About $5.7 billion in aid will be coming from the federal government, but even that vast sum will not restore the ravaged farms, homes, and businesses. Now that the dramatic events have passed, it will be easy to forget, especially since, even in the St. Louis region, only a very small percentage of the people suffered directly. As far as we know, the homes of only 16 of Washington University's 8,266 employees were flooded. The challenge will be to stay at the task until it is complete.

Recently, the Dalai Lama spoke at Washington University. He emphasized the goodness of human beings. In his view, hate and violence are aberrations of the normally peaceful human spirit; he believes that, in the long run, our better natures will prevail. One does not have to be a Tibetan Buddhist to be thankful that our fellow humans pull together in unselfish and altruistic ways. Among this year's blessings, I count those professionals and volunteers who worked so hard for their neighbors at the time of the Flood of '93.

I count also as blessings the friends of Washington University whose generosity and concern for others find expression in building a great institution of learning that contributes to the preservation and enhancement of civilization and to the education of a new generation of leaders. I am personally grateful to you and to others with whom I have had the pleasure and privilege of working this past year in this great enterprise.

May 1994 The right to express one's views, and the point at which exercise of that right impinges on the freedom of others, is a perennial issue on the campus of Washington University and our sister institutions. One frequently hears the term "academic freedom," which includes freedom to speak and write about one's beliefs no matter how controversial they may be.

Lately, there has been a great deal of discussion on campuses and in the popular media about "political correctness," sometimes abbreviated as "PC." Some have asked whether fear of offending individuals or groups leads to improper or even unconstitutional restraints on freedom of expression.

Recently, Washington University's student newspaper, *Student Life*, asked me to do a piece on freedom of expression. The occasion was that some students had chalked statements on campus buildings. They believed they were exercising their right to freedom of expression, while others believed they were defacing buildings. Since we have procedures for resolving such differences, I wrote a more general piece, which I think might be of interest to friends of our University.

"At Washington University, students and faculty can express their views without fear for their grades, their salaries, or any of the benefits available to members of the University community. Our University has a long tradition of defending this right. The mid-nineteenth-century charter forbids discrimination on the basis of religious or political beliefs.

May 1994

In the 1950s, when many universities caved in to pressure to dismiss faculty for political reasons, Washington University received national recognition for supporting the rights of those with very unpopular views.

"Thus, the University safeguards the efforts of faculty and students who seek to come closer to the truth and then report what they find. This protection, called academic freedom, not only serves the interests of the individual, but it also promotes the well-being of society. For new ideas are not always popular or well received, nor is it easy to tell which idea will pass the test of time and which will be proved wrong. We do know that, throughout human history, understanding and progress have been halted as unpopular views were suppressed and individuals voicing them punished and even killed. It is worth noting that it is almost always the powerful who suppress the views of the weak and the defenseless.

"Why then do some seek to institute speech codes or other limitations on what one can say? The answer is, of course, that speech can be dishonest as well as honest. It can harm as well as enlighten. It can intimidate, mislead, and sow hate. Speech can destroy trust and undermine community.

"So the question is: How can we uphold free speech and at the same time maintain our tradition of civility and make sure our community remains a place of openness, trust, and mutual understanding? Guatama Buddha had an answer that is still valid today:

'Lie not; be truthful.
Speak the truth
With discretion, fearlessly
And in a loving heart.'

"If we could all adhere to that maxim, no one would be tempted to write speech codes or impose other restraints. Of course, the last 2,500 years have shown that most people ignore the precept of Buddha most of the time, but the world is a better place because some try. If each of us were to do his or her best to live up to that standard for only a few years, we would set an example of an academic community that could inspire the world. I would personally prefer trying to follow Buddha's approach—responding to hate speech with the truth as I see it—rather than attempting to restrain someone else's speech. After all, identifying and debating important ideas and issues is part of Washington University's responsibility.

"It must be added that even academic freedom will not always insulate you from the personal pain that may sometimes follow the telling of your truth, no matter how gently you state it, no matter how loving your heart. Your friends may look askance; you may not be invited to a party or elected to head an organization. Reporting an unpopular conviction is not for the fainthearted. Buddha admonished us to speak the truth 'fearlessly.' To do so still requires courage.

"While developing understanding can be difficult and reporting painful, there are great rewards as well. Those who can see deeply into reality and have the courage to carry their message to others, have been and can be today among the greatest benefactors of our human race."

My contributions will, of course, not end the debate. We humans will always be wrestling with the extent and limits of our freedoms and of our responsibilities. To do so with civility and respect for the views of others is in Washington University's tradition and remains our continuing challenge.

August 1994 What follows are some summer thoughts stimulated by recent tragic happenings in the world.

Most of the time, we take our civilization for granted. We expect to be able to travel where we please, to have food when we are hungry, to be safe in our homes, and to be treated fairly or, if not, to bring complaints before an impartial judge. We talk with whom we want, when we want—and always without fear. All of these boons seem our natural right. Then we open the pages of our newspapers or turn on our television sets and see what happens when civilization breaks down. Starvation and sickness, terror and filth, suffering and death are epidemic. People are murdering each other for revenge and even for sport. We are horrified. We ask ourselves: Can these people be human, like us? Have they laughed and loved, provided for their families, and enjoyed their children? We know in our hearts that they have; we must conclude that they are like us.

Perhaps we think of the famous passage from John Donne:

"No man is an Island, entire of itself;
Every man is a piece of the Continent, a part of the main;
If a clod be washed away by the sea, Europe is the less as well as if a promontory were....
Any man's death diminishes me, because I am involved in Mankind;
And therefore never send to know for whom the bell tolls;
It tolls for thee."

Realizing its truth, we are suddenly forced to see a side of our species that we would rather forget. We learn what people can do to each other when hate and fear are loose in the land, and the normal restraints of civilized behavior have evaporated. People in the former Yugoslavia and Rwanda are human just like us. They share with us the same behavioral repertoire. Given the right circumstances, there go we—and who can say whether we would be the aggressors or the victims.

Civilization needs preserving; we all have a stake in doing so. The task is never-ending, for children are not born civilized, not our own or anyone else's. Each new child has to go through the learning period in the family, then in school, and finally, for those with the talent to be the leaders of tomorrow, in college. Some will go on to graduate schools; some will devote the rest of their lives to those callings that carry on the civilizing process. It all seems natural and simple—and most of the time it is, yet occasionally things go awry. The links of learning and civilization are broken. We need to continue to strengthen the barriers against such evil days.

Progress assumes that one will preserve civilized society, and it looks ahead to happier days. Universities contribute to progress in two ways: first, in education. Universities were founded to educate. Well-prepared young people armed with intelligence, energy, and understanding graduate into the world of work ready to make their contribution to the advancement of society. The second contribution comes from the scholarly and research ideas of the faculty. Talented individuals are given time and encouraged to take the long view, as they add to the store of human understanding and wisdom. The products of their work are studied and pondered by others, thus contributing to the flow of ideas necessary for progress.

Some may occasionally ask whether we have not had enough progress. Would it not be sensible to slow things down for a bit? Such a concern evokes sympathy, but to try to get along without progress is hardly realistic. Whenever we look at this world of 5.5 billion people, we see urgent problems that can be solved only with new ways of thinking and of acting. We must preserve the environment. The world's people need to be fed, housed, and protected from disasters. In this country, we desire to improve health while holding down the costs of medical care, to strengthen education, to provide more jobs, to control crime, and to eradicate poverty. We need responsible and responsive political systems. None of these goals will be accomplished without progress. We cannot turn the clock back to a simpler time; we can only move forward, meeting the challenges of our era.

Chancellor William H. Danforth with students at Homecoming, 1994

August 1994

One of the great privileges of working for Washington University is the hope of preserving and enhancing civilization and fostering civilized behavior. It is a realistic and reasonable hope. I thank you for being a part of turning that hope into reality.

November 1994 In this season of Thanksgiving—my last as Chancellor —I should like to thank you, the supporters of Washington University.

Thanks to you, the last two decades have been good for Washington University. You and I and many others have been about the task of building and strengthening an institution that has lasted for 141 years and should go on for hundreds more. As I see it, we have been giving back to a world that has treated us well, a gift that will preserve and enhance our civilization and will contribute year after year to the progress of the human race.

We have helped provide education for some of the brightest and ablest young people of the world, the potential leaders of their generations. Many are already involved in successful careers.

We have supported some of the world's most distinguished writers, scholars, scientists, and thinkers. Their work will guide people of this and future eras to learn more about the world and to better understand themselves. Their studies help provide the conceptual tools for better health, for preserving the environment, for establishing more just and humane governments, for feeding the hungry, for caring for the sick, and for many other boons.

We have aided those who reach into the community to give service to others: physicians, counselors, teachers, and consultants.

We have strengthened a University that will keep alive our ideals, hopes, and dreams for generations to come. We have, I believe, contributed to human betterment.

I thank you for being a part of this endeavor. Washington University could not be as great a University without you. You are examples of an important American tradition, of free people joining together to promote the common welfare. This tradition has endured as the world has changed. We are no longer just neighbor helping neighbor or friend helping friend. We are thousands of people of good will, spread around the globe, generously joining hands to create an international University that can serve as an example to the world.

I thank you also for your friendship and moral support year after year. You have taken Ibby and me into your hearts. You have rejoiced when things have gone well; you have been forbearing when things have gone less well than they should. Your friendship and encouragement have inspired us and sustained us. We could not be more grateful.

Together, we have accomplished a lot, but there is much more to do, as there always has been and always will be. Recently, someone asked me why Washington University had been successful. I answered, "Because we are never satisfied." Our institution will change a great deal in the future, for change is an inevitable part of life. Much that is excellent today will not be good enough tomorrow. To be worthy of its heritage, Washington University must evolve and improve in the future, just as it has in the past. One constant, however, I can guarantee: Friends and supporters will be as essential as ever—probably even more so—as government support falters.

I hope that Thanksgiving 1994 will be a time when each of you can count many blessings. Thanks to you, I can count happily both Washington University's and my own.

January 1995 I hope that 1995 is good to Washington University and to us all. Personally, I look forward to what I consider to be the last semester of my senior year.

I cannot often enough say "thank you" to those whose work makes possible this great University. I have been fortunate to be associated with you. Every year I am more impressed by the hard work, the imagination, the talent, the good will, and the treasure that go into creating and sustaining our institution.

The experience of being Chancellor is continually inspiring. I see dedicated individuals working from early in the morning until late in the evening. I talk with generous donors who give their life's earnings to further our work. One of our colleagues said to me the other day, "Don't talk about careers. I have no career. I have an important job that needs to be done." I am impressed by how many, like that individual, believe in Washington University to the extent that its welfare becomes one of their highest personal priorities. These people make our institution a very special place.

The readers of this letter will know their parts of Washington University much better than I do, but I wish that all could have my gratifying experiences. I have welcomed countless freshmen and their parents and learned of their hopes and anxieties, as two generations begin a new phase of life. Graduation—the culmination of that experience—is always fun, but the excitement for me is the sense of accomplishment and growth shared by graduates and families alike.

I have visited with alumni around the world and learned of the successes they have made of their lives. Frequently I am asked, "How is Professor Y? He (or she) changed my life." Invariably, I suggest that the alum write or phone Professor Y to report on what he or she has meant. I doubt that many do, but I wish that more would.

Often, I hear knowledgeable individuals in the U.S. or in foreign lands say, "Yes, I know Washington University. You have a strong department of..." or "Please remember me to Professor X, one of the leaders in our field."

Chancellor Mark S. Wrighton (right) and Chancellor Emeritus William H. Danforth after the Citizen of the Year ceremony at Graham Chapel, March 25, 2008

January 1995

Most of all, I am gratified to think that we are all part of an institution dedicated to being home to some of the brightest and most imaginative people in the world and to educating leaders for coming generations. I thank each of you for making this possible.

I believe that we are well positioned for the change of chancellors. Never have so many spent so much time thinking about the future and the choices facing Washington University. We have an exceptional faculty and very strong administrative leadership. We have been sufficiently prudent financially to have escaped the kind of crisis experienced by some of our sister institutions.

Our reputation continues to grow; applications for admission are climbing. Importantly, we have a culture that encourages people to work together across departmental and disciplinary lines, so as to make the whole greater than the sum of its parts.

I do not expect the coming years to be easy. The financial tides that have been flowing in favor of universities for 15 years or so seem to be heading in the other direction, as they had to eventually. But universities will go on contributing to human learning and understanding through teaching and research. Society will still support the institutions that do their jobs well. I am confident that Washington University will continue to enhance its stature. In the future, as in the past, the main drivers will be the talent, hard work, and good will of the Washington University community. That is why I have so much confidence.

March 1995 This final general letter during my Chancellorship will deal with change and continuity: more specifically, change and continuity in undergraduates.

Think, for instance, of the 1,250 women and men who will graduate this spring with a bachelor's degree. Most were born about 1973. (Some of their parents were undergraduates when I became Chancellor.) Happenings that seem to me to have occurred yesterday are to them ancient history. The last Apollo mission to the moon took place before they were born. In the year of their birth, the Watergate scandal broke, the Yom Kippur War was fought, and campus radicalism was on the wane. The next year, 1974, Nixon resigned from the presidency. When our graduates were two years old, Saigon fell to North Vietnam. Much of their knowledge of these events comes from history books.

They were four at the time of the Bakke case and seven when Ronald Reagan became President. They grew up in the television age of Sesame Street and Madonna, watching countless real and fictional acts of sex and violence as daily fare. Perhaps life imitated art, or art imitated life, as violence grew in the cities and in the schools. Opportunities expanded rapidly for minorities and women. They have seen an African-American run for president of the United States and a woman for vice-president. They have embraced new music and new styles of dress.

On average, the new graduates have read less and traveled more than their predecessors. Many have seen their families break up and re-form. Their attention span is shorter and their skill at calculating less well developed than in my day. On the other hand, they live with the problems of the environment, they worry about over-population, they volunteer to help the homeless, and they are concerned about equal opportunity for all. As pioneers of the information age, most are adept at using computers.

Although those graduating this spring have grown up with very different experiences from mine, yet much is the same. Undergraduates are still young human beings just as we once were.

They have the same incredible energy: They can go to an evening meeting, then party, then come back to their rooms to study until three in the morning, get up and go to class the next day, take an examination, and play basketball in the afternoon—all the while wondering why there is never enough to do.

They learn and adapt to new situations—physical and intellectual—at a dizzying pace. They experience the same excitement of moving on to a new adventure, of getting closer to life's work. Most still believe that they can improve the world left them by their parents and grandparents.

Importantly, students are, as always, searching for greater understanding, trying to come closer to truth, and seeking a lifestyle that is basically honest and in keeping with the way they see the world. They are trying to carve out niches for themselves and striving for meaning in the chaos that sometimes threatens to engulf them. Students continue to find love and hope and friendship—and perhaps even a bit of self-acceptance.

There is continuity in our response as well. Older people, like us, may look at the superficial differences in dress, music, language, and behavior, and say, "What's the matter with them? That's not the best way. We have it figured out better." There is nothing wrong with an older group saying these things. No one has a corner on wisdom, least of all the young. There is much to learn. Experience counts.

But each age, as does each individual, has to work out its own synthesis, or in slang terms, get its own act together; each learns to express its own values in its own way. Maybe the recognition of what is change and what is continuity, of what belongs to the moment and what belongs to our common thread of humanity, is the beginning of wisdom.

Certainly, it has been a privilege to share in the lives, the hopes, the ideals, and the dreams of young people who come to Washington University. I wish everyone could have that experience.

Thank you for your friendship and for your support of the institution that educates these wonderful students. I am sure that your contribution will have been a good investment, realized in the lives of these graduates who show great promise for enhancing our civilization.

Chancellor William H. Danforth and Elizabeth Gray ("Ibby") Danforth on her birthday, 1974

William H. Danforth, MD, served Washington University in St. Louis as chancellor from 1971 to 1995 and as vice-chancellor for medical affairs from 1965 to 1971. After retirement as chancellor, he served as chairman of Washington University's Board of Trustees for four years.

Dr. Danforth was educated at Westminster College in Fulton, Missouri, Princeton University, and Harvard Medical School. He trained as a House Officer of Barnes Hospital and St. Louis Children's Hospital and as a fellow at Washington University in Internal Medicine and in Biochemistry.

In 1950 he married Elizabeth Anne Gray, his life partner for 54 years, after whom are named the Elizabeth Gray Danforth Scholarship Program, Elizabeth Gray Danforth residence hall, Ibby's Bistro in Danforth University Center, and "Ibby's" Garden, all at Washington University. The University has also honored Dr. and Mrs. Danforth by naming the Danforth Scholars Program for them, along with the new University Center; in 2006, the Hilltop Campus was renamed the "Danforth Campus" in honor of Dr. and Mrs. Danforth, the Danforth family, and the Danforth Foundation. The Danforths have four children, thirteen grandchildren, and one great grandchild.

Currently, Dr. Danforth is chairman of the Board of Directors of the Donald Danforth Plant Science Center and of St. Louis's Coalition for Plant and Life Sciences. He serves on the boards of the Danforth Foundation, the American Youth Foundation, and the St. Louis Christmas Carols Association.

Like former chancellor Ethan A.H. Shepley, Dr. Danforth received the Alexander Meiklejohn Award from the American Association of University Professors in 2000 for his support of academic freedom. Washington University is the only institution to have two Meiklejohn honorees.

PHOTO CREDITS

pii Herb Weitman; University Archives, Photo Services Collection, People- Danforth, 94-474D-31

pIV Herb Weitman; University Archives, Photo Services Collection, People-Danforth, 71-232G-26A

pVIII Herb Weitman; University Archives, Photo Services Collection, People-Danforth, 73-290E-24A

p5 unkown; also published by Associated Press; University Archives, Arthur Holly Compton Personal Papers, Series 9, Box 7, 1931-1935

p9 Joe Angeles; University Archives, Photo Services Collection, People-McLeod, Jim, 90-449C-23

p15 Herb Weitman; University Archives, Photo Services Collection, People-Kassabaum, 78-107B-22

p17 Herb Weitman; University Archives, Photo Services Collection, Events-Alliance for WU, 81-554E-32

p20 unknown; University Archives, Robert S. Brookings Papers, Box 1, "Chancellor's Home Cecilwood"

p23 unknown; University Archives, Photo Services Collection, People-Cori, 76-32A

p26 personal photo from Dr. Danforth's collection

p30 Herb Weitman; University Archives, Photo Services Collection, People-Tao, Bill, 77-325-34

p33 Joe Angeles; University Archives, Photo Services Collection, Events-Special Olympics, 91-65C-10

p39 University Archives, Yearbook Collection, *Hatchet* 1942-43, page 22

p42 Herb Weitman; University Archives, Photo Services Collection, People-Thurston, Jarvis, 75-148B-28A

p45 David Kilper; University Archives, Photo Services Collection, Slides-St. Louis Scenes, Flood

p52 Doug Miner; University Archives, Photo Services Collection, People-Danforth, 94-473A-18

p56 Joe Angeles; Photo Services Collection, 2008

p60 Herb Weitman; personal photo from Dr. Danforth's collection. 1974